Into the

Willows

AuthorHouse™
1663 Liberty Drive
Bloomington, IN 47403
www.authorhouse.com
Phone: 1-800-839-8640

Published by AuthorHouse   02/07/2013

ISBN: 978-1-4772-8369-1 (sc)
ISBN: 978-1-4772-8371-4 (e)

Library of Congress Control Number: 2012920004

Into the

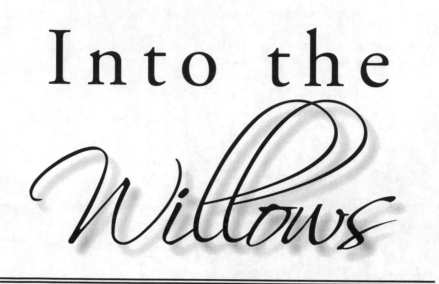

Willows

A collection of Poems by Devin Burke

Devin Burke

authorHOUSE®

Contents

Special Thanks

I would like to give a special thanks to Mary Bowman-Cline for the wonderful paintings she provided for this book. She is an amazing artist and a fantastic aunt. You have been there for me to watch me grow, and you have shared in another part of my life, my poetry.

Dedicated to my loving, caring, and supportive Mother, Debra. You are my rock, guide, and hero. Forever will I love you. And to my older brother Kyle. You will forever be missed.

"Poetry wasn't written to be analyzed; it was meant to inspire without reason, to touch without understanding."

Poe's Perfect Raven

With the night the wind blew, across the timid wet dew,
And the trees that knew, would never say,
Darkness becomes one with night, and with the moon of white,
And the trees of mighty height, and the dark drifts away,
The trees stopped blowing, and again the dark drifts away-
But the raven just sat there, with nothing more to say.

As I walk along I count the trees, as if there all a ring of keys,
All leading to a different door all leading away,
All with something new behind, something new to find,
But when opened I am blind, to the bird that lay,
And I watch the branch where the bird did lay,
But the raven just sat there, with nothing more to say.

Instead I walk past, knowing the stare won't last,
I walk fast as its eyes upon me sway,
Looking me up and down, looking at me with his devilish frown,
With teeth so brown, looking at the moon I pray,
And the trees stop blowing as if he can hear me pray,
But the raven just sat there, with nothing more to say.

All my years I've tried to be perfect, and all my fears,
Have all come true, in an imperfect way,

But I've come to see, there may not be, a perfect me,
And I've always wondered how to be, and I just have may,
Once found how, but I shall eventually may,
And I realize nobody will ever say.

People hide in their rooms, engraving themselves in imminent tombs,
They hide their secret of perfection, hide it away,
They hide in a place, where they think they'll find grace,
But they show in their face, they show how grey,
There no more perfect than thee, they are also grey,
And I think to myself "how" as I lay.

As I sit and ponder, my lost mind begins to wonder,
And I look into a lake covered by a musky grey,
The water is still but my ears begin to fill,
With sounds over the hill, and I look to where the raven lay,
As it yelps in the air from the branch where it lay,
And all went quiet, and sat there the raven with nothing more to say.

Now it all came clear, it had become my worst fear,
And I did shed a tear, as I thought back way,
As I remember, it was a cold long December,
While I sit by my burning ember, it was late in day,
And the raven was there, though the entire day,
The raven just sat there, without even a word to say.

With his eyes me he follows, upon the tree of hollow,
While I walk my feet pound as I walk to the bay,
Sand rolling through my feet, maybe the raven I must meet,
The mist lay over like a sheet, covering the waves as they play,
They roll and crash together all day long, the waves they play,
And the raven sit watching, watching without a word to say.

The lake began to freeze, as I look up at the trees,
The bird was no longer there, it had flown away,
It was gone, as the sun rose above the dawn,
He was fast, foregone into a glassy dismay,
When I looked back a figure appeared to my dismay,

And when I looked again it just went away.

Where did the raven go, why not to me he bestow,
I had questions that need answers without delay,
But no raven here, or no raven there,
I could not bear, to anymore decay,
Where was that fiend or bird, which let me decay?
Then there he was, with only one word to say.

One word he had said, as he sits on his icy bed,
His word in my head, as if I must obey,
I sit there to think, staring I dare not blink,
He had said "perfect", and then my mind went astray,
Did he know what I wanted? again my mind went astray,
Then the raven just sat there, nothing more to say.

The ice were he sat, is not even that,
Was not frost nor ice, no cold it portray,
It gave off a reflection, a watching collection,
But showed me the wrong direction, me it did betray,
As I looked I saw myself as perfect, it did betray-
And then the raven starts to say.

"Thou want to be great, but that not thou fate,
This frozen lake I sit, it will display,
What thou would be, I sat on that tree,
I sat all day just thou and thee, on the tree of hollow,
And I continue to follow, upon my tree of hollow."
And again the raven had no more to say.

And then I looked into the ice, hoping the vision would suffice,
I saw a perfect me, and in a way,
I no longer lust, to be clean off the dust,
And my mind began to bust, and then I felt a delay,
I need to be perfect; I wanted to be with no delay,
But the raven just sits there and nothing he did say.

Maybe the raven could, but maybe he is not good,

He can make me perfect, take my bad away,
I want to have not a single flaw, to live above man's law,
People to shout in awe then my life might be okay,
And if he could make a lake of ice, I had to be okay,
Just like that he had read my mind and began to say.

And again spoke the bird, as I listen and heard,
With his beak it moved as on the ice he stays,
He spoke with such grace, looking right at my face,
Speaking at a charming pace that I could not look away,
And more words, I still could not look away-
And then he continued to say.

"You want to be, or need to be so badly,
Why is perfect so great, why would it allay,
It wouldn't calm your soul, or fill that gaping hole,
Or let you extol what you have, your life would be grey,
Nothing more to want, or love, forever grey,
Sit here and listen to what I say."

"I don't know how to define, how exactly to be divine,
But I can tell you that I could perfect, but you will pay,
I could make you great, but what would that create,
Just another dark fate with a black dismay,
So I tell you to stay away, and not lead yourself into dismay,
Listen and thou shall live, listen to what thee have to say."

The raven that sat on the tree, and watched over thee,
The raven, the fiend or beast, has led me to obey,
He has led me to know, that being perfect is a fantasy so long ago,
And he is not enemy nor foe, as he showed me the way.
A creature created by Poe, sent to show me the way,
And now I know what to do, as I listened to what it had to say

3 Parts of Green Grass

1

Grass was once green,
Once lustful and bright
Once green as the trees,
And silent like night.
Once had flowers yellow as bees,
Had pollen to spread around,
No wind, just silence no sound.
Grass once clean cut and flat,
Surrounding a garden Nome where it sat.
Sun would shine off the Nome's head,
As it sat still on its grassy green bed.

2

Grass began to wither and rot,
As the sun beat, glazing and hot.
The grass was dying with no hope to survive,
It then realized it was no longer alive.
It now turned from green to grey,
And at that moment the green of the grass went away.

3

Now the grass was dead,
The smell the blood and dirt it shed,
It blew in the trembling wind,
As the cold froze even the strongest of kin.
The grass was now grey and black,
As the grass realized what it lack,
The grass no longer green, gone forever,
It turned out the grass wasn't really that clever.
And ever on the other side,
The green of the grass died.

Four Colors of Fire

One is red
Because it's like a dream
Came true as I lay in bed.
One is green
Because of the everlasting
Thoughts of my desolate queen.
One is blue,
Because of all the thoughts
Running through my head of you,
The last isn't really a color
It stands for the misplaced
And those who are lost.
For those thrown away like waste,
and brought upon a color.
The color black.
It is the fourth in a sequence
And the last piece of a puzzle.
Four different colors all the same
That come together to make,
A master piece, a flame.

A Devils Look

I look him in the eye
And he looked back at me
I couldn't help but cry
I couldn't help but plea.

I knew I was wrong
I knew what I did
He stared at me hard and long
So I ran to the closet and hid.

He was looking up and down
One two three four
Came a knock and a frown
Feet shown under the door.

Heart stops blank no beat
Light stops dead
I see his feet
Next his head.

Running past he grabs my leg
I trip and my knees bleed
I say "no" and mildly beg

No! no! no! my endless plead.

He hears nothing just looks
Analyzing my ever whine
As if reading a thousand books
But my soul is bound, it is mine.

So go away you beguiled beast
Go back to the fiery pits of hell
Tonight on my soul you shall not feast
Go back to where you dwell.

One two three four
As I watched him march
Back to his fiery door.

A Great Trickster

Say what you mean
You my innocent queen
Say as you please
As I bow down on my knees
As your loyal pet
As I am deeply in debt
Say what you need
As I sit here cry and bleed,
Taking away my soul with all your greed
And yet, I sit here and plead
For insanity
Yet you continue to beat
As me a symbol of humanity
Taking away all heat
You're so cruel
Think I'm a fool
To fall in such a trap
I did not fall
That I did not do at all
I was tricked
From behind I was kicked.
I look up still on my knees
Still continuing to freeze

And ask one more time
In this modifying rhyme
Let me go
And I'll finish the show
For one last night
To be a puppet I will not spite
Goodbye my long lost friend
Back to humanity I must ascend.

Two Parts to a Heart

A heart so torn in two
It never even knew
That it could be broken again
And shattered in the rain
Forgetting is the only way to heal
Forgetting how you feel
A heart that's been broken
So very unspoken
A heart is wrapped in tape
Waiting for its escape
Sewed together with lines of hate
Something put there by the hands of fate
It's been broken but never broke
To love again, that's a joke
It belongs to two people
Both alike in vein
Both to which I cannot explain
For some reason they are much alike
Both taken from my heart an endless strike
Both love for no infinite reason
Both feelings change as much as the seasons.
Two alike in soul
Both in my heart making a hole

To gather dust
And an eternal lust
Empty as the sky
As reassuring as good-bye
Hole to one day be filled
Or to be stabbed and killed
How to fix the problem is the question
From cupid I expect a confession
Of why he does this to our hearts
Is it his way of performing arts
Or his cruel little game
For winning he may proclaim
Or is it supposed to work
Because it came with one little perk
A hole in my heart.

Just a Myth

The rain begins to pour,
You're heart begins to sour,
Tears begin to fall,
Your eyes begin to see it all,
Truth is never a lie,
But sometime it brings a sigh.
Water drops on your lips and seems fake,
Feeling the entire kiss you take,
A moment to never forget,
You're minds eternally lit,
You decide, you make a choice.
You listen closely to their voice,
Have you ever wondered what if?
As your body becomes completely stiff.
How different your life would be,
Would you be freer?
And come back to me.
Or would you want to keep going,
Never truly knowing,
What could have been great?
Will you forever wait?
For us to be together
Our bond as thin as a feather,

What I am talking about
Is a moment no one can live without,
When your life flashes before you
Not you're past,
But you're future,
And who you see yourself with,
And you decide if it becomes just a myth.

Depth of a Poem

A poem is something we write
Something we come to know
It brings us a new light
But something we don't want to show.
It lets us write our story
No matter what it may tell,
Whether or not it is of glory.
Or a final farewell.
Love or hate, this does not matter
But if you chose love, your heart may shatter.
Hate on the other hand, hate is desire
It will spread through you like a fire
A poem truly comes from the heart
A game where there is no restart
An endless love song
Were words of life, truly belong
So a daring question is asked
And a poem to top them all is unmasked.
Does it tell of death?
Of our last single breathe?
Or of a time
Where loving someone was not a crime.
And poetry, although feared, was then respected

And the hearts and souls of most, it infected
It became known as a fall back
Something people could turn to when their lives were black
A poem is something that tells of you
Something you write when you are blue
Something to give us a new view
A short story of something so true.

A Poem of Time

How can we tell the time of day?
How can we tell when the past drifts away,
When the days drag on,
Seeming almost endless, completely forgone.
How can we see time, but in a word?
One single one, once long ago heard.
One that's been lost, forever gone
Dragged endlessly into the bleeding dawn.
How can we understand time, but in a machine,
How can we see something that's always unseen?
How can we tell whether its day nor night,
Or see into the distance dark or light.
How can we say we understand what's not there,
And come across something so rare.
How can we look at the hands of a clock?
When we can't even unlock the timeless lock.
How do we know it's real?
As it goes round and round in its ticking wheel.

An Abstract Art

This is a part of me,
Something for all to see,
These poems come from my heart,
I and my writing shall never part.
Poetry is an observation,
Something such as a star constellation,
You watch what it makes,
And then realize only a few
Are what they really are.
They only show the darkest of their heart,
Poetry is a musically thing, it is an art.

Aching, While the Wind Whispers

While the wind whispers
And the aching of my blisters
Continues in my pounding feet,
And the cold rust of my seat,
So longingly creek
And water from the pipes leak,
As snow slams against my door,
And dust crawls across my floor,
The cold of its metal stinging,
Sounds of the wind singing,
The thoughts of death,
Being able to see your own breath,
The imminent silence of being
The delusional power of seeing
The weight the world heaving in hand
The horizon slowly expand,
The sun begins to rise,
As the moon retreats, and dies
While the wind whispers,
And the memory and haunt follow,
And my shadowed heart hollow
As you fade deep into tomorrow.

After the World Ended

After the world died,
The sun also went to hide,
Time scarcely gone
No more night nor dawn.
No dirt just dust,
As the world wither and rust.
Not water just blood
No grass just mud,
Grass turned to stone
Nothing became known,
And after the end
There was no friend,
Because no one to meet,
No water or food to eat.
Only one stood tall
Above the rest, above all.
But all was not much
All you couldn't touch,
This man, he was alone
He was nothing, his own.
Wise old man, standing here,
He's watched it all disappear.
Watched it go by and fade

He watched as it was covered in shade.
And now he regrets the dead
And the road that lay ahead.
This wise old man, had a plan.
But now all is hollow,
Nothing leading to tomorrow,
Nothing but grief and sorrow.

Angels Creed

And now here we stand
Planning never to land
We fly through the skies
Telling people all our beautiful lies
We are loved very much
And yet you're hearts we never touch
We look down into a place of sorrow
With little hope for a rich tomorrow
We watch as the earth crumbles
And the truth of love fumbles
But now all we can do is sit back and watch
As the clock ticks on man's endless watch.

Sand Filled Tear

Along this sandy beach I walk
In my mind all we do is talk and talk
So along this beach I pondered
Into the gloomy night I wondered
The sea calls to me to take a swim
Into the gloomy ocean so grim,
The moon gives me light, a source to follow
As the water uptakes and I slowly wallow,
And the sandy beach takes,
As the waves and salt shakes,
The sound of the fish,
The silence of a swish,
Through me takes upon the watery sight,
Paddling into the oceanless night.

Beginning to End

It started in heaven, and ended in hell
As the middle of eternity rang its bell
They wanted to be together till the end
All along, time they were trying to bend
They wanted to be together till the end was over
So they wished all their luck on a 3-leaf clover
But they knew one heart would break from a deceitful lie
And the heart of them both let out a daring cry
They knew they have to live their lives
Because only without love the heart thrives
So they went on dates,
But the end still waits
And now the end has come
And they must go back to where they are from.
It started in heaven, and ended in hell
With their final breathe, they said their last farewell.

Bleeding Through

We all know
That when you,
Write with a pen,
It is permanent.
But did you know,
That a little goes through
To the next page.
Only a little, but enough
To see, exactly
What they wrote,
About thee.
And as the ink trickles
Through the paper.
It leaves a trace,
When you look at the ink
Left behind, by the pen.
What do you think,
Right there, right then.
The more you look
Can you make something out?
What do you think it is about?
A story perhaps,
Maybe about a place

Can you make out a familiar face?
So do you understand now?
That when you write with a pen,
You leave behind something that has once been
And when you're done
The words bleed through
One by one.

Carved in Stone

Our destiny is written in the wall
Holding us back in case we fall
Hope was meant to be,
But not for us to see
We watch as the world passes us by
Without even a chance to sigh
But sometimes we take that small leap
And end up in a slumber less sleep
For hope is a word simply to follow
But without it our destinies seem so hollow.

Cold of You

When I touch you,
Your skin is blue,
Cold frozen as ice,
You're tough so you stare.
So gentle so nice,
My soft hand,
Moves across you,
Like slick sand.
You lay ever so still,
Not a single movement,
Not even one.
As the moon shines
Waiting for the sun,
Your eyes open wide.
Staring into nothingness
Side to side,
Nothing across your mind,
No look no thoughts,
Nothing just blind.
Dead.

Darkest Color

Some say
That the darkest color
Is the color grey
And that could leave you in dismay
Because the way I see
The darkest color
Is me.

Day and Night

There are two things in the world the same
The day and the night are both one
They only have a different name
The moon and the sun.

The day seems to be kind
The night as reckless a beast
But if we do not find
The night will have finally ceased.

And if two becomes one
And we lose the night
And live with only the sun
With nothing more than light.

So for now one is still two
But the days get close, only a few.

Dear Heart

Dear Heart,
Beating in my chest,
My eternal guest,
The way you sing,
To me it's magic.
But it tells a story,
So lost and tragic,
The sound of a beat,
The blood rushing,
The intense heat.
You sing my thoughts,
You sing my soul,
You make me whole,
Beating in my chest,
My love stricken nest,
My eternal guest,
Dear heart,
You may rest.

Desolate Window

Through this desolate window I ache
As I stare into nothing and shake
The rain falls like angels creed,
As I wipe away the tears I bleed.

And the gentle and majestic rain
Only brings upon me sorrow and pain,
And the grey blackened skies only block my view
Of a sky I never truly knew.

The windows blackened and I see no more,
As my curiosity drives and I open the door.
As is opens I am filled with dismay,
Because there is nothing there, not even grey.

As if I am blind nothing appears,
Nothing more than my desolate tears.

Dream of a Dream

Dream into a night
That's not really real,
Look at a fire ignite
Into crimson and steel.

Dream into the sky
Where you soar
A place where you fly,
Where you roar.

Dream dreams so big
They make the world dark,
So large and glorious they
Make the moon twinkle and spark.

Dream of an enormous sun,
One that blinds the trees,
Until your dream is done,
As they blow in the breeze.

Dream of a meadow of mice,
Scurrying around a small well,
Then it turns to ice,

And the mice say farewell.

Dream of a mountain of snow,
With a river of thorns,
And perched above a crow,
With devilish horns.

Dream of yourself in ten years,
With a dog and a house,
Having gone through the tears,
And a loving spouse.

Dream of a reason,
One single thing,
Or of a season,
Warm like the delightful spring.

Dream of blue eyes,
That have a hint of grey,
Looking at you so wise,
In the mist of day.

Dream of heaven and hell,
Two different domains,
One you sing the other you yell,
One there's sun the other there's rain.

Dream of a dream,
Where you met me,
Dream of an ocean,
Dream of a sea.

Dream that I am the waves,
And play all through the day,
Now where both in our graves,
And the dreams have gone away.

Dream of a dream with no end.

Dream within a Man

I once had a dream
Of someone it might seem
Was lost, sitting in the dark
And I followed this man
As his journey began,
It starts with ink,
As it began to sink,
Into his blood,
It runs down fast,
Almost like a flood.
It started out
As he wrote without doubt.
I once had a dream,
Of someone it might seem,
This man I dreamed of,
He also had a dream, one of love,
And in his dream of love, was another,
And so it began, and dream within a man.

A Different World

What if all moments where grey
What if all nights where day.
What if all people where dead
What if all thoughts have been said.
What if all we know and love
What if all this is a message
From above.
What if all reasoning is doubt
What if all the people began to shout,
What if all we did was scream
What if all we knew wasn't what it seem,
What if all of it was just a lie
What if all of us where to die,
What if the entire world were silent.
What if the entire world weren't so violent?
What if all of man came together
What if all of us were weightless
Like a feather,
What do all of us have to blame?
For the fire and death inside our name
And what do we owe this occasion to,
What has become of our everlasting sky of blue?

Everlasting Dark

An everlasting dark
That has taken over my mind
But into it I must embark
For otherwise I am blind.
The light has gone astray
Mocked my life with such remorse
But with it gone the dark I must obey
Because my sadness, it is the source.
Every day I ask it to come back
The light that to return
Because love my life does lack
My heart, is my highest concern
So I ask you darkness, please go away
Leave me here in the white
For no farther can my heart stray
Here and now bring me light.
In my hearts endless flight.
I am the night, and the dawn.

Falling Darkness

When the night falls
And darkness rises in the halls
You're eyes become tired
And you're dreams become inspired
The sun goes away to hide
And the mood arises with pride
The clocks all begin to slow
And it becomes quite from far below.
Clouds begin to disappear
And waking up becomes our only fear
The mind drifts away
And begins to stray
The shadows aren't really there
And life seems to never be fair
You lose it all during the day
And find yourself in dismay
But when you're filled with dark
You feel that special spark
The dark brings out the good
Until the day is understood.

Forever in Ashes

The grains in the ash are small
They crawl through a hole as they fall
Cold wind blows through the sand
As it lay gently in my hand.
A goodbye is said,
A tear falls from my head.
The wind takes them away
To a journey on the oceans bay
Waves break them as they part
Into an ocean of a broken heart
Your body lays empty, lonely inside
Your body emits the sadness that you cannot hide
One less person for you to hold
It would last forever, you were told
These ash's represent what stood for forever
Who would have thought the devils so clever?
To trick a person into believing a story
And making them watch him take all the glory
Someday I will find you
And the phrase "hell froze over" will come true

I swear that to you . . . .
These ashes resemble the time we meet our fate
So when these ashes are lifted away
Don't be sad and let your mind stray
This just means they have lived there forever.

Grace of Words

Poetry is the motion of hand,
Swiftly up and down, side to side,
Never being known never planned.
It can be of love or those who've died.

Poetry can be easy and slow,
Made of words that rhyme,
Words of glass that are even and flow,
Like the winds of time.

Poetry can burn like fire,
Or freeze like solid ice,
Be born of raw desire,
Or as random as a 6-sided dice.

Poetry expresses the soul,
Words of the mind
Filling a wound or gaping hole,
Or cure the elder or the blind.

Poetry can mend your heart,
Bring peace to war,
Complete the part,

Of the day we bore.

Gives us a way out,
A place to go,
A place to shout,
Where no wind blow.

Creates a reality of infinite thought,
Unreal yet completely here,
This place we've so long sought,
Or a place we no long fear.

A dark that's really light
A moon that's really the sun
A day that's really a night,
And a poem that brought us as one.

Poetry is words of grace,
Elegant and calming our mind,
Bringing us to place,
Where harmony we may find.

Worlds suffer from torment and pain,
Rain crashes on hard ground,
Burning and burning like a flame,
As we find what we have found.

Poetry comes from a world of alone,
Bring us out of the dust,
Bring us back home
Away from corruption and lust.

Poetry is simply a phrase
Of grace and sorrow combine
Putting us in an endless daze
A burning ember of time.

Poetry is the motion of hand,
Never knowing, never planned

Hope of Men

All for nothing
Nothing for all
We bring tonight at this ball
Let the music be heard
And your happiness be reassured
For together we lie
Hoping never to die
We fight for what we could
Not for what we should
Awake we sleep
Alone we weep
Together we take
All that we must break.

House with the Black Door

I've always been afraid
Of the house of black,
The one that sat in the shade.

It was rusted and falling apart
Nails red with blood,
Red like a once loved heart.

I've never thought it would invite,
Me to come through the black door,
But on the other side it is white.

The inside had lights of gold,
And shined like a star,
It was warm not cold.

Even though the outside was dead,
Inside there was a window of diamonds,
And a statue next to a blue bed.

I was always afraid of the house of black,
Where the spiders are domain,
But now I see there just smiles,
No misery or pair.

If You Were

If you were the sun
I would be alone during the night,
If you and the sky were one,
I would feel warm in the light.

If you were the sea,
I would stand by and watch it all day.
If you were a part of me,
I would look in the mirror till it rusted to grey.

If you were the wind,
I'd let it blow through my hair,
If you were my skin
I'd never leave it bare.

If you were a ring,
I would wear you on my hand,
If you were to sing,
I would listen till the night end

If you were peace,
I would fight for those who cry,
If you made the world cease,

Id gracefully die.
If you were with me,
Then I shall live forever,
I shall live free,
To be sad never.

If you were a rose,
Id smell the petals,
Make a poem to compose,
And let it be great.

If you were to exist,
Than so shall I.

Key to Life

The key rests in a place,
Far far away,
Where the wind dances
And the sun flares
And the grass is covered
By a small wet dew.
To find such a place
Would be so great
It might just suffice.

Leader of Flesh

Every blood has its owner
And every organ has its donor,
Every moment has its end
And every wound has its mend,
Every person has their dream
But every time they die,
And every time we cry,
Every time for the blood.
Every blood has a path
And every equation is just part of math,
Every dinner has its toast,
And every party has its host.
Every night has its day,
And every spring has its May.
Every dark has its light,
And every person has their fight.
And every look has its sight.
Every blood has a heart
And every love has a start.
Every death has a birth,
And every fire has a hearth.
With so many thinks the same,
With so many with a different name,
Why are all people apart?
Where all our blood starts,
Within all our hearts.

Life

Life has a weird was of working things out
Leaves you with such little doubt
It gives you a blinding curse
Leaving things only worse
Every single day things change,
The way life works is very strange.
People say time mends our mistakes
But as time goes on, my heart only aches
so maybe those people are right
but for me it still hurts here on this night.
And I don't think it will ever end
My heart shall never mend.
Some people say live without regrets
But how can I do that when life just forgets,
That it left me out to die
It pushed me off the edge
Thinking I could fly
But I grabbed onto the ledge,
And I will beat this little game
I will be the one to put out life's eternal flame.
Some people say love is a cure
But I believe it to be a lure
Into something very dark
A much daring remark
But not matter what people say
In life, it's just another day

Life of a Tear

Here tonight I stand alone and tired
For my tears are much less than desired.
They begin in my heart
For only when I am not being smart
Migrate to be born in my eye
For it happens when someone tells me a lie
Live their lives on my cheek
Making themselves known very sleek.
As they roll down they die on my lips
As my life soars on as sailing ships
Tears come and go
And my love for you it does show
For now I leave you with just a goodbye
For my tears say I am to shy.

Little Red Ball

A little red ball
So far from us all
Up there looking so small
Looking down upon me
So that from the night
We shall be free
To wage our final fight.
Our planet thrives on its existence
Despite the great distance.
We look up to see nothing but red
But inside we are really dead
Were meant to look beyond
This shallow pond
Of water so bright
And the sun it shall ignite

Lucifer

He sits behind his desk of fire
Waiting for us to make a move of desire
He waits in his eternal sleep
Waiting for us to make a single peep
He knows of our love and hate
Sitting there eating off his fiery plate
One bad choice and we'll be there
His torture and hates he's willing to share
There is nine circles all of death
Were you'll die if you take a single breathe
His gates are open, and he's letting us in
For this is a game we shall never win.

Man's Destruction

We are nothing but all
Destined to fall
We take away all hope
Leaving man at a downward slope
In the beginning we were scared
And now we are feared
We take all for granted
On this terrestrial planet
And now is our end
For this planet we must mend.

Maybe

Maybe a night is really a night
And a day is really a day
Maybe the sun isn't really as bright
And it shines more grey.
Maybe if we look one at a time
Each glance up in the light
We wouldn't have to make up this rhyme.
And all shall be alright
Maybe love is just a saying
And it really means sadness
It's the reason we keep on swaying
And just brings upon us madness.
Maybe, just maybe one day, It will change
And things may not be so strange.
Maybe. We will find our day
And relinquish our night
And fly away!

Memorizing

Why is the ocean so blue?
Maybe it's just a reflection of you,
Because blue stands for love
And a thought of you comes from above.
Where do waves come from?
Have you ever heard a whale hum?
You do know that they sing
Just listening is memorizing.
Mist lay bare among the sand
As the grains fall through your hand,
You look off into the sun
You lose your mind in the fun
So have we answered why?
The color of the ocean is so shy.
So lastly I can say goodbye
And go back to where I lie.

Mind of a Dream

I dream of a day
When bad in the world
Will forever go away.
I dream of the color red
Of the dark within,
I and the millions dead.
I dream of a parade of black
With cars of gold,
But diamonds they'd lack.
I dream of a sun,
That would forever shine
Then my dream would be done.
I dream or true love,
One we cannot describe.
And of a beautiful white dove.
I dream of a reason
Of why we are here
Of why the changing of the season.
I dream of a rainbow,
One of colors galore,
While we listen as the wind blows,
I dream of the sea,
With waves that play

One of ice to forever be
I dream all during the night
Then I awake to the blinding light
And all of my dreams go away,
As I wake to my unwritten day.

Missing piece

I feel an empty abyss of sorrow
A longing for no more tomorrow,
A piece missing in nothing but rain
A piece not there causing agony and pain.
I feel complete and whole but lost,
I feel drowsy and still cold with frost,
Standing alone with you not here
Wishing upon a magic trick,
One where you shall appear.
Something from me is gone
And I'm waiting on the dawn
That may never even come,
But the sight of the dawn makes me numb,
Breath escapes my very soul
As it burns like embers from dark coal,
You take away my gaze
And entrap it in your beautiful maze.
I feel gone and misplaced,
But now with this beauty I'm faced
To come clean and tell
I love you and I've fell,
Your heart has pulled me in
And your smile has brought me a grin,

Even though I don't have you yet
I am no longer upset.
I thought I was missing a piece
I thought I would cease,
To live or die,
To fall or cry,
But I was very wrong
Cause you've been right here,
In front of me all along.
I was once a broken puzzle,
But you have put me back together.

A Mothers Grace

Breathing in air,
Twirling bright hair,
Today is not a day,
The sky is blue not grey,
It is a celebration for you,
You're why the sky is blue,
You make our worlds collide,
We stand side by side,
As a family in grace,
As you hold together
Our tenderness space.
A chore or two why the fight,
As we rest unwitting into the night.
We should be nicer more sublime,
We should thank you for our wonderful time.
You have granted us with a life like no other,
We could not have asked for a more perfect mother.
You're more than human with the things you do,
You've watched over us as we've grew.
I love you to death mom and always will
And we will always love you and Bill.

A Mouse and a Crow

There was a mouse in a field
Afraid of the sun, using trees to shield
His fear of the beast the blazing sun,
So he hid in the grass and became one.
Why is the mouse so deathly afraid?
Why does he cower? And hide in the shade.
As the blazing sun across the weather
And the mouse came across a feather
It was black, one of a crow,
As the thick clouds cross ever so slow.
Then the crow came out to say
"do not be afraid, let your fright go away"
"But the sun is so scary,
It makes my little heart weary."
"But the sun had done nothing wrong,
It sit up there, were it belong.
"But if I come out to say hi
There's the little chance I could die"
"No worry little mouse, the sun will bring you no harm,
So come out to play with me on our grassy farm."
So in the end the mouse came out to play,
And is still friends with the crow to this very day.

Music of the Heart

We listen to the songs that say what we feel inside
But in my heart those songs have died.
I don't deserve the bliss of their sweet voice.
To love and feel this pain, that was not my choice.
I didn't make the decision, to fall in love
But this problem of mine is something I don't talk of.
I don't deserve to own my heart
From my body and my mind it must part.
I have thrown it away, buried in the ground
To the heaven and hell it is bound.
For love is something we don't control
Something we want to through in a deep hole.
What is love? People always ask.
But when we find love, it is always hidden behind a mask.
It is unknowing and comes fast.
But before we can see it, it has passed.
It has never truly showed itself, came out of its hiding place.
Because this is something man will always chase.
The point of it is unknown. We shall never know.
So for now we just go along with the flow.

My Dark Place

Alone in this place
This place of dark
Alone here
Where I lark
And this place
Where I am
I am alone
Forever
Dammed here to die
To be imprisoned
To forever cry
But this place
Where I sit
And dark I trace
This is mine
And for now
It'll do just fine.

My Grey Sky

Why is the sky always so grey?
And why won't the grey just go away.
Is it only grey to me?
Is it that no one else can see?
Will the grey go away some day?
Or up there does it forever lay.
This grey sky is blocking the moon
I don't believe it will go away all too soon.
So what do I do if my sky is never blue?
Do I continue to stare?
Never knowing how much I can see.
To look at my grey sky
All the way up there, so very high,
All the way to were my grey lies.

My Guitar

On my guitar I play these songs
All telling a story of where my heart belongs
My songs I wrote of sorrow
Finding a place in your tomorrow
Some songs are soft, ease your mind
Others are dark, hard to find
When love meets my hand, the notes just come
But when they reach my lips, I begin to hum
These notes are lyrics of my heart
Some may even say they are a form of art,
When I play my mind drifts away.
I try to leave but people beg me to stay.
I describe life, but in the sound of my guitar
Some say my talent, came from a star.
A single note starts the spark
And bring your hearts out of the dark.
But my music will eventually end
And you will begin to find a new trend.
I set down the guitar and leave the stage . . .
As my heart crawls back into its eternal cage.

My Story

I'm here to tell you my story,
So that others after me will know.
The truth about forever,
And the lies told from below.
Worlds were hope was never.
A world where there is no good
Only a few rebellions lurked in the night
And here they stood
Tangled in an endless fight.
So there you have it, a world of pain
But a story, that must be took in vein.

Not a Day

Not a day goes by,
That I cease to cry
And my soul strives to die
And time, it passes my eye
Time begins to slow and everyday becomes a years,
And every ocean becomes my tear,
And every night becomes my fear,
And as I watch the passing of every day,
As it lingers and drifts away,
As it fades and turns to dust,
Inlaying all to the night its trust,
Not a day went though
As the clouds cover the sky,
But only a few,
Not a day goes by,
That I don't look at the sky,
And wish I could fly,
To leave this place,
To forever bury my face,
In the dust of the dead
To make forever my bed.

Purgatory

I am here
But I am gone
I shed a tear
But I do not cry,
I bleed
But do not die.
I swim in pain
Alone and cold
With no name
I am neither a ghost nor ghoul,
But simply a person
A stupid fool
I stand beside you
But you feel nothing
You wonder who
Could be watching
But no worries no fear,
I am not me, I am not here.
I move my eyes
But see none
I hear the goodbyes.
But they're not to me,
Because I am not real

I touch but do not feel
I have so long bleed,
But for some reason
I am not dead,
I cry and weep
But am awake
Cause I do not sleep.
I live every day,
But lately,
They've been slipping away,
Fading more black and grey,
Fading like the sun
As dark and light become one.
I drift into the unseen
Against the wind
I sit down to see
I still am not here
I am nothing but me
My hair blows in the wind
But makes no sound
It stays upon me
Forever bound,
I am here
I am nowhere,
But for a moment,
I feel life.

One Day

One day when the clouds where high
And the wet soaked ground turns to ice,
Dark and grey rolled over the sky
And dark scattered across like mice.

On one day blood ran through the streets,
And filled the sewers with red,
As we listen to our own heart beats,
And trees die as they wept and bleed.

On one day time it froze
And the icy wind no longer blows.

One Day a Raven sat on a Hill

One day a raven sat on a hill,
Slick black feathers and a sharp bill.
Sat upon rocks hotter than the sun,
The hill and the raven became one.
It just sat there all day,
Even as the sky turn to grey,
And all the blue went away.
Rain poured down on the raven
Clouds with thunder and fire,
As gods spoke of lust and desire
One two three four,
Bolts of lightning thrashing floor,
One strayed from the pack,
Protection the raven lack,
It hit him without warning
He lived and stood tall,
He began to grow no longer small
His eyes got black and he grew a tail,
His stubby feet grew white and pale.

Devin Burke

A horn came out of his dark little head,
As his eyes darkened and became red,
He grew fists from his chest,
No longer was the puny raven not the best,
Spikes began to grow on his back,
As the bolt receded to its pack,
Now the raven sits on the grass,
Watching the changing storm as it pass.

Our Day

Today is today,
And not yesterday.
But still a day
No matter what you say
It will always stay,
Just a day.
So as we lay
Upon this hill,
Sitting tremendously still
Thinking of today
Looking out upon the bay
What comes from tomorrow,
Is nothing but sorrow.
So we lay in wait
For another passing of time.
Upon this hill we ponder
Into the days endless wonder.

Puppeteer

I am just a puppet
And you my puppeteer
When you want, I shall disappear
My life Is controlled by you
And a show so very untrue
The curtains soon open to begin the show
And a story of love so long ago
A soul entrapped by enduring love
And a single trick with a white dove,
Trapped forever as this puppet, in an unfair game
This string on my back put me in shame.
Could I cut myself loose?
I can't bare anymore abuse.
For my puppeteer is cruel
And makes me look like a fool.
Once my strings our off I can begin my life
But for that I will need a very strong knife.
For the strings of love cannot be broken
By three little words so lightly spoken.
But someday these strings will break
And from this undying nightmare I shall wake.
Into a new life to begin
And the puppeteer will emerge from within.

Raven for Love

If I had a raven bird,
I'd name it the first thing I heard.
It would be magnificent and pretty
And light up like a grand city.
Its feathers would be softer than skin
And it would soar gently though the wind.
It would have eyes of red,
And fly over a grave yard,
That was harvesting the dead.
It would be able to do tricks,
Or build a house of nothing but sticks.
It could be nothing and disappear,
It could make a minute seem like a year.
It could make water shine,
And the hairs stand on my spine.
It would fly and fly all day
I would let it fly free,
But it never went away.
I could watch it soar through rain,
It would turn upside down like a plane.
It sometimes talked to me in the night,
But I'd be asleep by the fire,
As it spark and ignite.

It would whisper dreams it had,
Sometimes I could tell in its voice,
It had been troubled and sad.
But I always thought it was not real,
And the raven in my dream may heal.
This was the best raven ever,
And I wished to keep him forever.
But even as I watched it play,
In the sky, the sky of blue,
I think all day,
Of trading him, for you.

Room of Secrets

In that room
There she lies
In that rooms
A dirty secret hides
Written on the glass
Water soaking in the grass.
A message for her to read
About a story of an endless creed
Telling the truth about a heart
In there lies a secret art.

Sad Day, Good

One day in a year
One day always to fear.
A day meaning being closer to death
Closer to that final breathe.
But it's a day you want to be thought of
It's a day when you can choose all of the above.
Most say it's the happiest day of the year
I disagree, because it can also bring tears.
When you realize no one even knows
And how much they care begins to show.
It is the saddest thing on this day
But there is one thing to make this go away
When you hear someone say
Happy birthday!

Seasons

Emotions are an interesting thing,
They come and go like the seasons.
Most of them are pointless, come without reasons.
Some are like the winter, the cold and snow
Some come from a time long ago.
The snow comes down like tears
As the emotions thicken like years.
Others like the summer, heat and swimming,
The love of a lost one dimming,
A time for moving on,
Finding yourself a beautiful swan,
A princess to make your own,
So now your emotions won't me alone.
Emotions can also be like the spring
Flowers growing and trees standing tall
And the sun shines bright if I do recall.
And our emotions get tighter
But the sun shines no brighter,
As time drifts into the fall
When our emotions in all,
Began to go back down,
And again the seasons,
Only bring upon us frown.

Shadow in a Painting

Painting a picture, all in grey,
A picture of poor and gold,
A picture of our dying day.

Picture of black and nothing more,
Of dark cloaks and shaded men,
Of a black cat lying on the floor.

Picture with shadows to fill the room,
Shadows that collapse on walls,
Shadows filling our desolate tomb.

Dark climbed up the chair,
Like a spider then fell,
Like winter willow so long bare.

Red joined the mixture of paint
It came to design a fire,
It could see the light oh so faint.

The paint melted into something surreal,
Black and red mixed together,
Black undoing a story so real.

Devin Burke

Brush decided to put out the flame,
Grey again was there, nothing else,
Grey now wrote on the wall a name.

The picture was of death,
Dark and symmetrical view of hell,
Dark tales of our aching breathe.

A picture of hell display,
Where fire burns like suns,
Where the diseased and dead lay.

Painting a picture, one of hell,
A pictures core in which we dwell.

Shall be Lost, Shall be Found

Shall be lost
Shall be found
Thrown and tossed
To the dirty ground,
Lost in a maze
An endless phrase
Lost in my gaze
A maze of sorrow
We were put in here
To live for tomorrow
To live forever bare
To live for more
We shut and locked the door,
And laid in cover on the floor,
We live for the great
We live to look
Were here because of fate,
From you we took
We live to be
We live to see
We live because of me.

She Again

And another time has come
And she again, has won
And again, I am done.
I have walked off the edge
Pled the endless pledge,
To no longer live nor die,
To truly see through my own eye,
Straight through the sky
Sky of grey and dark
A sky with a spark,
A beginning to an end,
A lover and friend
From heaven they descend,
To complete the sky of grey
To stop it from decay,
Again her revenge has agreed
That I deserve to die and bleed,
I deserve to lie in the dirt,
And let blood trickle down my shirt,
And cry out for hope and salvation
A cry of absolute desperation.
So again she wins and takes it all
One piece at a time until I fall.

Single Kiss

What is a kiss?
A kiss is poetry in motion,
A long loving emotion,
A single dove in the ocean,
And the trust of one's devotion.
It explains the unknown
Let's us call someone our own.
Makes us feel not alone.
Makes our hearts completely blown.
It's the way we see life
Appears as an endless strife
And a kiss, will make you complete.
A kiss can make you hear your heart beat.
So what is a kiss?
Something lost in my endless abyss.
Or is it the love of an angel's bliss.
This . . . . One . . . . Single . . . . Kiss.

Single Moment

Stepping out in the cold air
A feeling so very rare.
Heart doesn't miss a beat
You can barely feel your feet.
Some say it's the greatest game
But I just want them to remember my name
I don't step out onto the grass for a win
But to prove something to myself within.
Moons huge, control your eyes
You let go of all the stupid lies
And for that moment nothing else matters
And all that you knew shatters
You feel free wishing to fly
And everyone one else you defy
And that whistle blows
As the moon still glows
But in a flash it is done
And there is no more fun
Just smiles or tears
And come back the fears.
The moon goes and hides
And the morning around the corning, it resides.

Sky of Red

A sky of red,
That's so long bleed,
Up there rotting and dead,
Someone once said,
A city of blood,
Wiped away with a flood,
Gone for now,
Never knowing how,
Not there, filled with blue
All thoughts of a never ending you.

Something to Live For

So if I were to say
I wanted to live no longer
Past this day
Would you become stronger?
And tell me you wouldn't let me
And you'd hold me down
Until I agree
To wipe away my frown
What if I were to say I didn't want to smile
And if I were to say living isn't worthwhile
Would you ever care?
That I could no longer bare
To stay here on this earth
And die for what it's worth,
Existence itself is too much
But sometimes people's hearts
It can touch,
And their love it starts,
But what if no one cares
And all I have is tears,
Everyone has something that they live for,
Something that helps them soar.
But is it possible to have nothing,
But a pen and paper.

Story of a Man

This is a story of a man
And a tale of his life.
So this is where he began
Holding in his hand, a knife.
So it goes on
A wordless person
So very long forgone
As it starts to worsen
It begins in the morning
As he is asked a question
He wishes there was a warning,
Do you like me? And there started a long obsession.
The first date was at her house
And he almost kissed her
And her beautiful green blouse
But she did prefer
To not go that far so quick
So they hugged and said goodbye
And his heart started to grow thick
But that quickness would lead to his cry.
Their first kiss was at a movie he will never forget
And yet
He regrets that day the most

For now he is haunted by this ghost.
That winter they had so much fun
He never wanted it to be undone.
Spring came and still all was well
Then things quickly began to excel
But her friends were not willing
To let her go
To them that thought was chilling
So they moved very slow
To get her away
And their plan worked well,
As she began to stray
And he began to dwell.
He still remembers that rain day
When she said she no longer wanted to stay.
And that's the end
My dear old friend
Some say it's a love story
One of old glory,
Others a horror
Of a wondrous explorer.
But on this exploration he did die,
But he will never deny
That is was the best time he'd ever had
Although it made him have an everlasting sad
He still says he loved every moment of it
But to this he shall never admit
So there you go
With this story I must bestow
He was just a boy
But now the rest of his life he may enjoy.

Stupid Little Boy

Stupid little boy,
Full of a life without joy.
Thrown away like a toy,
Asked to obey,
To what he say,
Torn and broken
Like his words unspoken
Mouth sowed shut
Told never to speak
Looking for a retreat
Freedom he seek
From denial and pain
Living a joke in vein
Shaking in fear,
Wiping away his tear,
Letting it wonder and disappear,
Shadow of a man
Traced upon his hand
Door in the distance creaking
And quietly you can hear his weeping,
As he sits there and cry
All he does is try
And the shame he can't hide
Who lived by his side
And soon it will die,
For this stupid little boy no long cry.

Surprised

We were surprised,
To have found
Such a soul
To a human it's bound,
We'd never of guessed,
That if, we could find,
And to be so blessed,
Or forever blind.
As the day went through
And snow turned to water,
Wind began to blow
And dying became harder.
Because no one wanted it
It didn't seem to fit
Living a long life full of joy.
And just being thrown away like a toy,
They look to science,
To live forever
To make an alliance,
But they were not that clever
So we finally died
And I promise you this.
We never truly tried
And I lay upon a kiss
For us to share
And pass through the air.

The Castle Beneath the Snow

Once upon a time
Along long time ago,
Over the bridge and past the mute mime,
Behind the mountain and under the snow,
And behind the mountain and beneath the sky,
A beautiful desolate castle of gold and silver lie.
It was surrounding by a single rose,
A place nobody knows,
Dormant by mountains and covered by light,
A place with just day absolutely no night.
Where there is neither misery nor pain,
No storms no rain.
Behind the mountain,
And beneath the sky,
Under the snow and in the castle
Lies a princess with beautiful gold locks,
Who sits beneath unticking clocks,
Wearing glass shoes and dresses of white,
Dancing quietly in the absence of light.
While the record spin round and round,
As notes fly free in the nothingness of sound.
And a blind rabbit sit on the hill,
Watching the space where music must fill.

And the deaf bird who sits on the tree
Listens to the music like waves in a sea.
And the prince who's both blind and deaf,
Looks at her, stricken by his loss of breathe.
He hears nothing but knows she there,
As she dance softly to music while he stare,
Although he's blind he can see,
Like the flying wingless bee.
And he sees her here,
Saying "Oh my darling dear",
As she continues to dance in the hall,
She slips on the slick floor and fall,
Moving fast he caught her mid-air,
Smelling the diligent fragrance of her hair,
And he kissed her on the lips,
Holding her dauntless body by the hips.
But when he looked in her eye
He began to cry,
For she there did die,
And so he convinced himself he would see her again,
So he joined her in the graces of heaven,
And the unticking clock,
And the blind rabbit,
And even the deaf bird all mourned their deaths
But did not cry for they are now together,
Forever and ever,
And the clock started to tick,
And the rabbit started to see,
And the bird started to hear,
But most of all the prince got his love,
Where they now slumber up above.
And so a love story of every lasting woe,
In the castle beneath the snow.

The Castle on the Other Side

You've all head
Of the castle of light,
Where days a must
And it's never night.
Where the princess and the prince died,
But have you ever looked to the other side?
Where grass slowly dies,
And musky black water lies,
Where the sidewalks have no end,
And the paths twist and bend.
Where the sun never shined
And the slaves are all blinded.
And trees die before they're born,
And a heart broke of a sun so scorn.
Where the moon is domain,
And it constantly rain,
Where air is thick as blood,
And ground is nothing but mud,
Where pain and misery control,
And the air will blacken the soul.
Your feet will blister and bleed,
You'll strive for the comfort you most need,
And get absolutely none,

No light, no sun.
There is another castle that lay,
Upon a bed of black sand,
One of black and grey.
Surround by desolate thorns,
The diseased and dead they scream,
No princess recedes here, just a red man,
With a fiery tail and staff at hand.
Horns made of dusty bones,
Of men who've died and their blood moans.
No breeze, no wind,
Just dust that pierces the skin,
Dead trees lay bare,
Not a single leaf could be found
No green only black,
Inside the red man controls
And let those in
Who have once committed a sin,
Letting them burn forever.
Not just hell but much more,
This castle is darker,
And has been here long,
For those of corruption and wrong.

The Darkest Room

Breathe suddenly freezes
In dark clouds of rain,
Death larks in mysterious diseases
In the form of misery and pain.

Cracks in your mind,
Fragments pushing toward able subjects
Eyes playing tricks eyes are blind,
Pieces of a puzzle too perplex.

An old lady sitting in a chair,
Wearing a black cloak,
And curly black hair,
Whispering words that turn to smoke.

Owls perched on a tree above,
Heads turned one eighty degrees
Confined in them a single dove
Screaming in pairs of threes.

Blood rivers run down walls
Eventually reaching a black spider
Crossing its feet as it crawls,

Your alone and cold with no hope.
This is the darkest room,
A recreation of Devil's hell,
This is your tomb,
This is your cell.

Lie awake for now its dark.

The Dreamer

A shadow that climbs up the wall
And a heart that hopes for it all.
A dream that took over the mind,
And eyes of a lover so vividly blind.
A fairy tale forever followed
And the hope of one man swiftly swallowed.
Holding together tightly, forever locked
And a fantasy so unknowingly mocked.
But every dream has its last thought
And every lover has a princess they have sought
But for this lover is was only a dream, something not real
So happiness and joy this lover shall never feel.
A lover's heart with an arrow through it
And a game this lover has decided to quit
But dawn has come
And as he looks back at him dream he realizes it was dumb.
Because she is no longer here
So why waste such a glaring tear.
Maybe it's something he longs for
Maybe the dream is the only thing in life he can truly adore.
The sun only blinds his way,
But the moon he always asks to stay.
Because the moon brings her to him
And the sun takes her away . . . .

The Dusk that Beloved the Mourn

The dusk
In my definition,
Is a place
That illuminates your face.
It shows off your pretty smile.
And the rest begins to pile.
Your elegant green eyes,
That you know have never told lies.
They sometimes turn brown
As your face recedes down.
But no reason to hide,
Because those have also never lied.
There's a glow around you,
But its not new
Its now that the dusk lets me see,
What has always been around thee.
It shows me your beautiful hair,
That to look at, I cannot bare.
And its beauty is just too much
That just a single touch
Will do,
And it's the lucky few,
That is blessed with your beauty.
You are my mourn,
And I am your dusk.

The Dying sun

One day the world came as one
As we wept over our dying sun.
As it falls into a billion pieces,
Until one day it was gone and ceases.

We stare into the sky all day,
"Maybe it will come back" we say.
We pray to the sun that was once here,
As we watch as the stars shine like our tears.

One day the world watched in dismay,
As we watched as our sun went away,
And people where filled with fear and awe,
Confused about the death they just saw.

But now we sit in dark and wait,
For our sun to come back and return,
And brighten our world with its great,
And to, in infamy, us it shall forever burn.

One day our blazing sun went to die.
Somewhere in the universe, restless where it lie.

The Legacy of You

Pain and sorrow is our world now
Love and nurture it will never allow
Destruction and conquer, that's law
Without even a single flaw.
This is the world we live in
This is the world we know.
A world or pain underneath our skin
And people putting on a daring show.
But as we began our redemption, we came to see
That the world is so far deep, it's at a single knee.
We tried and tried for centuries to follow
But this world's future began even more hollow.
Our good deeds just led to death.
So eventually it came down to one last breathe.
It was time for our final act
The surface of the world was so badly cracked.
This was a show to remember
Like a fire's final ember.
Into our futures we rode
And to a world of pain, love and peace we bestowed.
So our world was once corrupt, death was bound.
But the world's real purpose we have finally found.

The Light in my Dark

You are my soul,
You are the light,
To fill my dark hole,
And continue through the night.

You make me feel
You make me see,
You make me heal,
You are me.

You are my grey,
You are my name,
You're the light to my day,
We are the same.

You're just as sweet
As the moon in all
As hot as summer heat,
And as colorful as the fall.

You are like me,
You are unseen,
Yet you can see,

The moral being.
You are light,
And I am dark,
You take away
My endless day.

Fifteen Years

The morning begins you feel old,
But as you reflect on the memory and gold,
Of the childhood greats and time,
I sit here and make you this rhyme.
You're a great person from what I know
And your beauty just continues to show and show.
Happy birthday forever and now,
Any enjoy life as long as it allow.
This morning you felt alive,
Now you're a one and a five.
Fifteen years of age,
What a new time and stage.

The Nazi's March

As we hide in our hidden room
Under the floor and beneath the broom
As our finger tips glisten with ice
Slightest sound would scare even the mice,
And we freeze and shiver
As our prides lessen and wither.
And our hands tremble and shake
For if they find us our families they'll take.
A violent knock comes at our door,
But we keep silent, here under the floor.
We hear the door break down.
As I look to my parents who's beginning to frown.
And pounding steps come from above,
"Oh come out come out my dearly love"
We hear the throwing of furniture and breaking of plates.
The Nazi's have come to determine out fates,
We all have a star on our shoulder that marks us as one.
But we're more than just that, we have come together like the moon
and the sun.
And suddenly all seems quite, all content,
As we listen and wonder through our listening vent.
Then all our hopes were immensely high,
None of us knowing we were about to die.

And still all is quiet, and we hear nothing at all.
Then all our hopes began to plunder and fall.
As light shinned in, blinding our eyes,
The Nazi's have found us, surrounding us like flies.
So it is in our hidden room where we all hide,
And together this is where we all died.

The Old Tinker

The tinker was old,
And sat in a withered oak seat
Winters were viscous and cold,
And summers were blazing with heat.

The tinker wore cloaks of grey,
And his hair was pale and white,
He worked on his clock all day,
And continued through the night.

The tinker had seen much,
Sick children bleed to death,
Butterflies land with a graceful touch,
Babies gasp for a single breathe.

The tinker was intelligent and wise,
His clock was silver and gold,
In the middle laid two eyes,
So he could watch time unfold.

He lived in a mountain of snow,
Where light shined down,
And the flakes would glisten and glow,
Upon the clocks and the town.

Hundreds were assembled and made,
All the hands going back,
Until time began to fade,
And reality started to crack.

His final clock was almost ready,
He needed to place one final piece,
His hands must be still and steady.
Then time just stood, ended and cease.

Time began to rewind fast,
Passing year by year,
Digging itself into the past,
Time began to disappear.

Wrinkles went away,
And the tinker regained his youth,
His hair turned brown from grey,
And for the first time in ten years he saw a tooth.

All the clocks were set,
And time rewound,
No remorse or regret,
The past was found.

The tinker was now a boy,
And he held the clock in hand,
Tears rolled filled with joy,
He did what he had planned.

The tinker was made of diamonds and jade,
And smiling he burst into ashes and began to fade.

The One

You make me disappear
Take away my one single fear.
My world becomes a daze
An endless maze
That without you I couldn't find my way
And would be lost for eternity
Without my guardian angel to guide me
I could not see
And so you make me feel complete
Something I would always want to repeat
So you are my everything
Sometimes making me feel like a king
Cause a king has all
And without you I'd fall
Into a dark abyss
So that's why I need your soft gentle kiss
More deceitful than Santa's naughty list.
This time, my heart. Is something you haven't missed.
And cupid I thank for that
Because happiness is where I'm at
And I will remain
Until that deadly rain.
And with it comes pain

That's when we won't be together
But that will be as some say "death do us part"
So is this were we start?
Are you going to say yes?
Or am I going to have to guess . . . .
Cause I've always been bad at chess.
But I must confess.
I think you're the one,
And so our endless romance has begun.

The Path with no End

As I walk down the path with no end,
As it twist and bend,
It's dark and long,
Light from here is gone,
The grass on both sides is dead,
All life from here has fled,
The path itself had died,
The end has gone away to hide,
The path is broken and cracked,
Love it did there lacked,
Trees lay overhead,
As they wept and bleed.
They cried out to me,
As I walk on the path and fall on my knee,
As I peer forward I see no door,
So I sit there weeping on the floor,
And the fact there is no end, has come to a close,
As the frosty wind blows,
If you look you can see the light
Look there, its shining so bright,
But the light is fake,
As the path continue to wind like a snake,
As the path with no end it has fell,
It is simply a place that represents hell.

The Red Man

There is a man
A man of red
Why he's red
Is because of a world
That's so long bleed
And is now dead
And to believe someone had once said
The world would soon change,
No longer be abnormal and strange
Would be foolish, and not considered right,
But the red man must watch
As the world bleeds into the night
The red the mans covered in
What we consider to be twin
To the dead and the alive
The worlds chaos, it uses and thrive,
he is covered in the blood of those who've died,
and mourn the deceased and those who've lied,
and the more the world crumbles and withers,
the long the blood on the man causes shivers.
There was a man
Once a man of red,
But the worlds so badly bleed
He has now drown,
Dying upon his face, a frown.

The Soul of my Shoe

The soul of my shoe
Has seen very few
Places here
Or places there
It does not travel
Across the dusty gravel
It does not go anywhere
Does it no longer dare?
To travel the land
Like it had planned.

The White Tree

There is a white tree
That lay above me
There is a white tree
That lay beside thee
It is not black nor grey,
But white on this day
And the sun shines upon it
And upon me as I sit
The wind blew,
But not at the tree,
Leaves would drop, but only a few,
At least from what I could see,
It's not always white, it would change tomorrow.
Only bringing upon me grief and sorrow,
But for today the tree is white
And the fact that it will change I cannot fight.
So I will embrace today,
Until the white of the tree goes away.

The World Bleeds

A wolf sits
In the middle of nowhere,
Shuffling leaves,
Dark cold winds,
The world bleeds.

The wolf is blind,
Nothing but black,
A little grey,
Trees would blow,
Knocking against one another,
In the dark of night,
The world bleeds.

The wolf is deaf,
Only the rustling of bushes,
The shine of a star,
The creation of life,
In the deepest abyss,
The world bleeds.

The wolf listens,
To the desperate pleads,
Of small people,
Put on a monolithic world,
Full of green and wish,
And an abandon place,
The world bleeds.

The wolf is alone,
Possessed by strings,
Shaped into a heeding puppet,
Dancing around in a void of nothing,
With a burden to hold a meaning,
But perpetual nature begins,
The world bleeds.

The wolf feels weak,
And slumps down to the grass,
And the world is broken,
Like millions of pieces of broken glass.
Fragments of blades,
Jagged and rippled through time,
And time itself ceased,
The world bleeds.

The wolf is dead,
No longer here, now gone,
Departed from the blood,
And the deceased world,
And its bladed grass,
And it's alone wolf,
And its puppets of sorrow,
And the hope that brings,
No tomorrow,
The world bleeds.

Twisted Relations

Two different people. In an alike world.
Two emotions violently swirled.
Together they became, closer than heaven to earth,
In an imminence rebirth.
There was no such thing as love here
Cause all love brought was our joined tear.
It was the emo and the jock.
Both adjoined by cupid's unbreakable lock.
Until one day both there misfortunes came true
And there relationship together began to look blue.
She had betrayed him, done him wrong,
This was the end of their beautiful song.
They went their separate ways.
An emo and a jock, what a daring phrase.
Two different people, in a corrupt place
Both of which have lost cupids race.

Under a Tree

Every day I wonder why
Sometime I even cry
What did happen that night?
Because to me it felt so right.
Every day I go on wondering
Just sitting there plundering.
Making up stories in my head
Stories that would leave one dead.
Under a tree in the day
Looking up to see a cloud so grey.
The cloud makes me think
Makes my heart fall into sync.
With the rhythm of the clouds
And the people in the crowds.
The entire cluster in our mind
In there it's tightly confined.
But still I can't let the question go
It's like a curse from below,
Testing my every wit
Like I'm a winning twit
But the shade of the tree

Devin Burke

Helps me to be
Cool and content
So my heart it does not torment
Under this tree.
I sit and think
With not even a single blink.

Untouched

Sometimes don't you wish someone cared?
And your life they shared.
Can you ever imagine yourself in a better place?
Don't you wish you could just once, win the race.
Maybe one day cupid won't be so mean
Someday our love for someone won't come unseen
Hearts will no longer be pieced with arrows and wood
And we can make a stand for what's truly good.
Will love always have to be a secret, something to hide?
And this pain won't have to be shared worldwide.
Some people say love isn't that bad
But then it's obviously something they haven't had
Cause it's better to have loved and lost
But really? Then at what cost
I think I'd rather now be sad everyday
And go on and live my life its own way.
Cause love does suck
And if you endure it, you have really bad luck.
I wish there was a time machine
Cause then I'd go back to before I was a teen.
Become unborn
And so violently torn.
So people ask every day. Is love worth the pain?
Go ahead. Just don't take it in vein.

Valentine's Day

One single day
Our hearts no longer sway
We come to know people as they are
Leaving your love as a tenderness scar
Understanding their love for us
No longer having to make a fuss
A day of no fighting
A day of endless uniting
One single gift, a red rose
Along with a letter, of love is does compose
A box of chocolate perhaps
To your heart, it leaves us maps.
This day two become one
And an endless romance it has begun
By the end of the night
You will be holding them tight.
But on this day one thing begins
Two endless grins
One single day
Where love is the theme of life's play.

Waiting

Waiting
People sit around
Looking for what they haven't found
All day and night
They look for something out of sight
High and low
We look, for something we do not know
But what are we looking for?
What is it that we need more?
Is it even out there
Is it past there here?
And into our own fear.
So we sit and wait
Hoping on a count of fate.
Waiting . . . . waiting. What if were waiting for something that will
never come
Something that we cannot become,
I believe we are waiting for love
Waiting to descend from above,
But love isn't real
It's something no one can feel
Because it's really just a curse

We Ended

Everyday
Is the same day
It never changes
In any way,
No matter how you look
At the way you see
Your eyes took
Away from me.
Time stands still
It's all the same
You lose all will
This is what the world became.
It's no longer good
This is where
It stood,
And the air
Stopped blowing
Plants stopped growing,
It was all the same
Leaving only us,
To blame.
And thus,
We ended.

When I Look at Your Eyes

When I look at your eyes
Your eyes of blue,
Ones I wish
I forever knew.
My mind wonders
And I believe I can fly,
For your eyes,
Are like the sky.
Bring joy when I see them
Brightens up my day
Just for the moment when you blink,
And for the second they go away,
I begin to think,
They might never come back
But they always do.
If I was granted one wish
I would ask to see your eyes forever
For then I could live forever happy
And be complete and want nothing more
But to see you and your eyes galore.

When the Dusk met the Dawn

When the dusk met the dawn
And the moon met the sun
And night became day,
The birds sang a song.
The soldier put down his gun,
And the musky fog rolled away
The sky became clear
And the moon came up
Followed by the sun
When the dusk met the dawn.
Life grew faster and silent,
Rolling by like a rock in a stream.
Moon said to the sun,
"Look at what we've done,
Made a better place from scratch"
"Look at the trees,
The way they blow,
Or the flowers,
Or even the bees"
Said the sun.
And they talked
Over the good and the bad,
No more night they said,

No more day.
And a crow chased a butterfly,
And nothing in the world could die,
It was perfect as far as they could see.
But something was wrong,
The waves in the ocean did not play,
There was no spring winter April or May,
No snow to fall or rain,
Although no misery nor pain,
The green plants enjoyed the rain,
The soldier starved and became old,
And the birds lost the will to sing.
And this perfect world that could not die,
Couldn't prevent us from being able to cry.
The soldier begged for death,
The plants begged for rain,
The birds begged for a breathe,
One single note to sing.
The crow gave up,
And the butterfly was no longer full of color
Leaves fell in nothingness of air,
Deserts became cold,
Mountains small,
A sea turned to sand,
And the sun frowned.
"what did we do,
were not meant to be,
Are you blind?
Can't you see?"

Things started to die,
The soldier
The plants
The birds
And the crow and the butterfly.
"I know see sun,
What here we have done,
Creating blackness and death,
We must part to restore order"
"goodbye my moon,
My everlasting beauty"
And they parted once again
Making a night, and a day,
And the world had to repair,
Restarting is the price we must pay.

When the Night Truly Ends

When the night truly ends
And time and reality bends,
And trees grow legs and walk,
And hands freeze on a clock.
When the creatures come out to play,
And the sky spirals with grey.
A bird grow horns from its head,
And its eyes turn from blue to red.
When the dark turns to light
And the day runs from the night,
Men cower in their brick houses
Holding their shaking spouses.
Hiding in basements of steel
Hoping it's a dream and not real.
When the night truly ends
The world between us transcends.

Whisper in My Ear

I hear a whisper in my ear
To turn around and see only my fear.
I see nothing standing there
A cool breeze going through my hair.
The hair on my back stood tall
As I turned around toward the wall.
Such a scary place
The dark, as it crosses your face.
Your heart begins to race.
It's like a person is born
And the old one is torn.
I hear a whisper in my ear
As I listen to my rolling tear.
It's like the world goes silent
And everything beings to seem to violent.
It's like a shooting star
You only have a second to wish, isn't it bizarre?
You know it won't come true
But you still hope the whole time through.
That the whisper is just your heart
Telling you to make a new start.
But whatever it tells me to do
I follow it right to the end of you.

Why the Light

Why the light
Why so bright
Why awaken me
I am blinded cannot see
Why the light
That awakens my day
Just go light
Go away.
Why do you torment
With your tremendous power
And cover me in light,
Where has it gone
Where is the night
Has it gone somewhere to hide?
As light makes its way inside
Why shall I be awaken
From my internal slumber
And dreams swiftly taken
Why light
Do you bother me so?

To the day I rue and no longer know
To a unforgiving sun
To crimes of blastfamy and mischief
Night is quiet and peaceful
My day is only my night
So I ask why light
Would you take away?
My nightly day.

Why the Sky

The sky is beautiful thing of blue,
And I've always wondered why?
Then I was told it's because of you.
It wants to be beautiful and shine,
It's god's magnicifant design.
It was built to shelter you,
Then it just grew and grew.
it was built to intend a place.
Where your mind can escape in grace.
The ocean was also made,
As a gift for you to observe,
As the soft sand sparkles ever single nerve.
Without you it would turn to grey,
And take away some part of the day,
That we honor and commit to knowing,
And the blue would forever stop showing.
Why is the sky blue?
Because of a god that loves forever you.

Wishing Star

I wished upon a falling star
I wished upon my endless scar,
When I wish I had said,
I wish the star will fall,
Upon my head,
I wish for the world to grow
I wish for the dull to glow,
I wished for the dark to shine,
I wish for poor to be divine
I wish for hunger to cease,
And for the world to finally have peace.
I wish of love of no measures
I wish for the greedy to lose their treasures.
I wished about our death
Together we take our breathe,
And hold it tightly, never letting go
Never faulting or though,
Just me and my star,
As I wish upon its glory
And tell of its story.

Wise Old Man

Wise and smart
But weak at heart,
A wise old man
Who once had a plan
Now alone
And never known.
Name soon forgotten
A place he lives so rotten.
This old man has come to see,
And he will always agree
The hatred found
Upon the ground
And grass and rocks
Un-openable locks
In these places
This old man has seen many faces.
And to summarize what he has seen
The grass is no longer green,
Nor on the other side.
Is it green, the grass has died.
And with it took a piece,
And right there
The earth did cease.

And the old man stood there bare.
Trying to understand
How the world could be buried in sand.
But it wasn't his fault
He did not make the world halt.
But instead man did as one
And into the dawn
They crushed what we once had
And there people stood still.
It wasn't gods doing
He had nothing brewing,
Not him, us
And thus
In the history books
It's not the way it looks
They will tell of death
Telling of our last breathe,
But who will they blame.
One single name.
And not tell the truth
And so the youth
Won't know what went on that day
When the earth began to decay.
But this old man knows the story
And will tell it not for glory
But for people to see
Exactly why he fell to his knee
And began to plea.
Wise and old
Sitting there in the cold
Old not by age,
But from rage.
And the day the earth did cease
Took away the final piece.

Cold December Day

I'm sorry to say
On this cold December day
I'm leaving you in dismay
And I look back
On what I've done
And count my poems
One by one,
They each took a while.
As they make my grand pile.
And they look at me,
As I look at them,
So empty
They sit there
To them it is not fair
They lie there bare
And sometimes I think
To myself
Why did I use so much ink?
To express me.

Before the Wise Man

There was a wise man,
But there was also a before,
Without the wrinkles on his hand,
And to offer something more.
Once a little boy, so small,
Who was forced to see?
As the world crumbled and fall,
And no longer cease to be.
And the days would come and go
That time would pass ever so slow,
It was as if the whole world was dead,
All asleep, still and silent from toe to head.
Smell of dead animals, and the sound of cries.
They were grey, mostly black were all the skies.
No clouds lingered there not even one,
Even away and gone was the sun.
So the little boy grew up with this,
But this, he shall never miss,
He grew up very fast, learned many things.
And even had time to stop and listen to the birds sing
But he also was able to watch the grass grown green,
But also was able to see the unseen,
Inside the before, in this time this place
And his courage of this young man's face.

Defying Death

As the time came for us to go
We stood there, hearts beating fast,
And without hesitation said no.
The man dressed in all black on a horse
Raised his eye brows to wonder
For no one has ever said no before.
Behind him sat a boat on fire,
Surrounded by bats and spiders,
And nothing more.
He said "we have to go,
What will happen if we don't I do not know"
But we stood there and politely said no.
"If I must I will take you by force"
"Were going nowhere" said we,
Don't you understand who I am?
The devils' sun and if I must
I'll take you one by one."
"You may try but you shall fail"
"Your beginning to wither, you dead
The hair is falling off your head
Just come follow me
I have for you a dying bed."
"We don't have to die not right now,

Not us not we we'll stay for now,
Leave us alone to rot
Are souls are stone and diamonds."
"Fine, die here on this boastful rock,
But I will be back some day
And until then I shall go away."
As the time came for us to go
Our hearts rattled among our chests
And we defied death
By simply saying no.

Fear Me

Fear me
If you are brave and courageous
Fear the sky
If you hate the rain or sun
Fear the stars
If you can't reach their beauty
Fear the dark
If you lust for light
Fear the sound of music
If you long for a heart
Fear planes
If you don't want to fly
Fear the night
If you hide from the day
Fear me
If you think you could
Over everything else
And it will all go away
Fear me

The Universe with Just one Star

If a universe had just one star
One shining in the mist of night,
Would you find it irregular and bizarre
If it never shined bright.
It cowered because it was alone,
Wising to have a star friend
The star was made of stone,
And lasted till the very end.
Of course there were many suns
All that lived for thousands of years,
But there were special ones,
Ones that could disappear.
But they soon would die,
Once again leaving the star to rot
And be gone without even a good-bye
And blow up on spot.
Now that was left was the star and some moons,
But the star is made of stone,
And so it wouldn't die,
Outliving the moons that drifted into the unknown.
Now there was nothing but the star
And the simple fragments
Of a once lived scar.

And the star would eventually fade
For the thought of being alone made it afraid.
So the star broke into many parts
Scattered like a million tiny hearts,
To other universes where there were more
For this little star to explore.

I'll be your slave

I'll be your slave for one whole day
If you promise to never go away,
I'll tend to you every will and desire
Feeding your heart like logs to a fire,
I'll take on any ruthless task
Your loving mind comes to ask,
I'll climb any mountain or cross any river
Or sit in the cold until my soul begins to shiver,
I'll swim across a never ending sea
As long as you're on the other side waiting for me,
I'll count to one billion and eight
If you promise me one single date,
I'll build you a pyramid or a marvelous arc
Or capture the sun to keep you from the dark,
I'll wait till the very end of time
For a glimpse of you being mine,
I'll paint you a mural the size of the sky
If you promise never to say good-bye,
I'll stare into your eyes until the very end
I hope to be with you all very soon,
But first I must find you the moon,
A prize for someone who's worth the win
And our never ending love's time to begin.
I'll be your slave for one whole day
If you promise to never go away.

The Widow's Tomb

Silent room screeches its rage
Entombed beauty lies dead
Scorched with time and age

Death comes quick to blind
Tears full of salt and water
Infused in the lost widow's mind

She stands in the webs and dust
Darkness dances in her shadow
As it starts to wither and rust

Screaming bloody cries
Are let out in silence
From the lost widows eyes

Alone in the screeching room
She's trapped forever by herself
In this widows tomb.

The Woodchips

Kids play,
And laugh and smile,
Night and day,
Oh glorious moon arise,
Comes and goes,
Away the goodbyes,
Tomorrow again,
Kids play more,
The woodchips glow,
Through the kids hair,
The morning wind blows,
They grow up and leave,
But the woodchips stay,
All night and day.

The Neverless Vision

A gleaming light
Of sorrow and dusk
Entwined my mind
Into melted rubber
Flowing from all directions
Rivers and lakes of thought
Light blasting through a window,
Covered by shadows of shade.

The River of Snow

Dark pebbles flow
Down the deep waters
Of the river of snow
And roll and roll
Tumbling among each other
Over one and another
Finding their way along
The deep river of snow.

The Oldest Sorrow

The first of one,
And beginning of the begun,
The oldest of all,
The longest call,
For safety and sorrow,
For the end of tomorrow,
The first cry,
The first falling tears,
From a saddening eye.
The first of all years,
And the end of minutes,
Seconds continue on,
Through the very first dawn,
The first sunset,
The beginning of regret,
The start of crime and war,
The end of murder and gore,
The oldest sorrow,
Bring forth a new day
For us to take away.

Magician of Souls

Agree with the idea of a town,
That works all day round,
That works without a sound
Using hammer and nail they pound.

Agree with a black grizzly bear,
That has dark golden hair,
That has prey hell never share,
Using teeth to shred and tear.

Agree with a man, who's wise and old,
That has many stories he's told,
That has wondered through many the cold,
Using the cane of oak he hold.

Agree to be a magician of souls
And conceive yourself to engage in their goals.

Rose of the Old

A man walks into a grand ball,
Takes off his hat he's too tall,
Away the coat made of animal fur,
Still too hot, he's not sure.

King above a grand crystal light,
Helping illuminate faces in the night.
His eyes begin a search of fate,
But the night carries on and gets late.

Panic consumes his long thought mind,
He has one soul to find.
That which has marvelous blue eyes,
And his gaze continues and fly's

Through black hats and rugged faces,
From sparkling glasses to unfound places,
But yet a hope ensues to drive,
To keep but a piece of him alive.

Then comes fourth yet a rose,
His old dying heart nearly knows,
To follow the scent of a flower,
Under the lament glow of fates shower.

Silhouette

Upon a shattered break of rain,
Comes a sense of the insane,
And laid upon the sky,
Does come a vague figure defy.

All bliss and sanctity is then thrown away.
Dark concern with the mindful day,
Grand silhouettes nightly home,
Does fourth the figure come all alone.

Upon a mellow red day,
The obscene figure lay,
Constructed by the stars light,
Does dampen man's delight.

Upon a time we hope to wait,
But for long the sky turns late,
And the sky remain the same,
Upon the figure in the rain.

Upon the minds of the insane,
Comes fourth our silhouettes sinful pain.

Never Knowing Hope

A black square lay upon a decrepit floor.
But a glow of time or of lore,
Separates the square from hence more,
Minced with cracks and homely tore.

The square solemnly sits alone,
Never stepped on never known,
Never even glanced with a thought,
For lonesomeness is the prize it's always sought.

The black square has no name,
Never in agony, never in pain,
By dim light and shallow fame,
All but faint glimpses of hope to blame.

But now the square is called hope,
All it has now is to bellow and mope.

Past's Treasure Chest

Underneath the sewer,
And beneath the bridge,
Forever away,
Where the water lay.
Where the wastes ride,
Upon boats of trash,
As it glide,
Upon our worries.
This is where it stays,
Forever away,
It never play,
Only black water.
Have you been to the place,
Where kindness meets greed,
Where the dreamers feed,
Where lost hopes confine,
And a north star,
Never shine.
Have you heard of such a place,
Where a golden locket falls from a hole,
In your pocket,
Forever away.

Where old friends are gone,
Blackness dispels the dawn,
Nights only to come,
To a wasteful slum,
Forever away,
Where it may stay.

?

The black curly cue,
That never knew,
Atop a black dot,
A tiny confused spot,
Sings a song,
intensely long,
With no real chorus,
That has no meaning,
No real plot,
As it sits alone,
Upon its lonesome dot.
The confusion queen,
Completely serene,
Mindfully mean,
Parking itself at the end,
Of a long thought sentence.
To conclude an idea,
But give no answer.
So if you come across,
This tiny question mark,
It might bite your mind,
Like a shark.

Or perhaps run away,
Leaving you in dismay.
It will always end,
With this curly,
Black bend.